# Discipleship or Deception?

*A conscious reality to the condition of the Church*

Samiour L. Patterson

Discipleship or Deception
Copyright © 2017 Samiour L. Patterson

For One Purpose Publishing
P.O. Box 2681
Frisco, TX 75034
ISBN 978-0-578-19221-5
Library of Congress number: TXu001671842
Reach us at: www.discipleshipordeception.com

Printed in USA

# Table of Contents

## Where we are

## How we got here

## Where we must go

# Acknowledgements

To my Lord and Savior Jesus Christ. For giving your life so that I may have life. For modeling and being the perfect example of a Servant Leader; and for granting me the privilege of being a small part of your great and divine plan of discipleship. To You be all of the Glory.

To my beautiful wife of 20 years, Christene – Wow, first for your faith in God, your belief in me, your ability to love me beyond my imperfections, your dedication, encouragement and your sacrifice. For all of your wisdom, and efforts and input included in this great work. You my Love, are my Good Thing. – Proverbs 18:22

To my wonderful children – Dominique, Darius, Christina Simone, Christopher Samuel, and Caelyn Summer – For being such beautiful gifts from God and having such beautiful hearts thanks for your never ending encouragement and belief in your Dad. Love you all.

To the two people who represent the greatest influence in my life, James & Louise Patterson my father and mother. There are no words to describe how grateful I am for the impartations that you have made in my life; For the sacrifice, love, provision, guidance, direction and most of all for Life. I love you dearly.

Now To all the great leaders, that I call heroes that have served and influenced me on this journey as my Pastor(s):

*Acknowledgements*

James Patterson - for your unbelievable wisdom, impeccable example of Holiness, and your unselfish ability to share, provide and encourage opportunities that allows me to sharpen my gift.

Dr. Alvin O'Neal Jackson – for your ability and dynamic creativity that compelled a struggling young man to submit to process and plan that God had for my life.

Dewayne Hunt – for your insight and teaching anointing that challenged me to desire a deeper more intimate understanding of God's Word.

Bishop T.D. Jakes – for your ability to inspire, encourage, coach, stimulate and motivate me to aspire and crave the More of God.

Randy Freeman – for your heart for outreach and the life changing opportunity provided to me to be a part of something so great.

Conway Edwards – for your never ending desire to make His Name Great and your ability to think strategically and model great leadership in our culture.

To my life group co-leads Tony and Treasa Bowers – for your endless love and dedication to our friendship that allows us to not only lead together but actually live life together. For your servant hearts, and your input, accountability and efforts spent in helping us to complete this great work. Love you Fam.

To my life group family – for being the family where we can be vulnerable, transparent and real as we do life together. Priceless!

# Foreword

*Then Jesus came to them (His Disciples) and said, "All authority in heaven and on earth has been given to me. [19] Therefore go and make disciples of all nations, baptizing them in the name of the Father and of the Son and of the Holy Spirit, [20] and teaching them to obey everything I have commanded you. And surely I am with you always, to the very end of the age." - Matthew 28:19-20*

A foreword is traditionally written by men and women who have gained a level of authority, influence, honor and respect in the culture. Because of their level of influence, these individuals are usually sought out by authors to endorse their body of work and share from a relational perspective, their thoughts of the author and the subject matter that the author has written about in the pages of their book. It is with no disregard to the many great leaders who have and continues to have influence in my life that I have elected to forgo tradition and simply emphasize and invoke a "Foreword" given by the One who has "All Authority" in the culture as well as in the cosmos. Given the essence of the message and content that lies within the following pages, understanding of my position behind this decision to invoke His Authority and influence will be very clear and suitably justified.

# Preface

*Discipleship - One who embraces and <u>assists in spreading</u> the teachings of another.*

*(b). an <u>active adherent</u>, as of a movement or philosophy.*

*Deception- The act of deceiving; <u>the state of being deceived</u>.*

*(b). something that deceives or is intended to deceive; fraud; artifice.*

One of the most fascinating areas to read in the bible are the four gospels of the bible is the four gospels of the New Testament (Matthew, Mark, Luke and John). It is here that we get to read about the miraculous birth of Jesus, His growing up, His earthly ministry, as well as His death, burial, and resurrection. While there are many amazing events, encounters, and revelations that unfold throughout the pages of the gospels, I have always been intrigued by a particular passage of scripture in John's gospel Chapter 14 and verse 12. It is here where Jesus is talking with His disciples about the way to the Father, to Phillip in particular and He says these words. "Believe in me when I say that I am in the Father and the Father is in me; or at least believe on the evidence of the works" that I've done. He then declares something so powerful that one cannot help but pause and ponder could this really be true? In verse 12 he states, "Very truly I tell you, whoever believes in me will do the works I have been doing, and they will do even greater things than these, because I am going to the Father." Wow! What a loaded statement. This would mean that those who follow Christ and believe in Him should not only be doing the works that He did (healing the sick, giving sight to the blind, raising the dead, feeding those in need, making disciples, etc.) but even greater works. I find it difficult to believe that anyone could read these verses and not be forced to ask the questions: Why are we not doing or seeing this happen in our culture

today? What could possibly be the cause of the absence of
such manifestations within our churches today? Could this
be a biblical error? Could Jesus have been lying? We
even have a natural tendency to accredit and justify Jesus'
abilities to have done such great works to His divine nature
and therefore (whether conscious or unconscious)
rationalize that we should not expect as much. However,
we must consider and be reminded that Jesus who was
God did not utilize His Divinity to His advantage but instead
was able to accomplish His ministry as an ordinary man
servant by being humble and obedient.

> *...Christ Jesus: [6.] Who, being in very nature God,
> did not consider equality with God something to be
> used to his own advantage; [7.] rather, he made
> himself nothing by taking the very nature of a
> servant, being made in human likeness.*

[8.] *And being found in appearance as a man, he humbled himself by being obedient to death—even death on a cross!* --- Philippians 2: 5-8

We also know that our Lord and Savior is not a liar nor is the bible in error. With that understanding, it is imperative that if we are ever to see and experience the full manifestation of Jesus' Promise (THE MORE OF GOD) in John 14:12 that our emphasis be focused on the significance of being humble and obedient and assuring that we, like Jesus are submitted to doing God's Work, God's Way.

I choose to believe that most leaders in the church start with a genuine desire to see God's people brought to maturity, transformation, discipleship and ultimately empowered to do these great/greater Works. However, in their quest for accelerated growth (numbers) and the mass needs that accommodate this type of growth, they allow their methods to maturity and discipleship to dissolve into movements of motivation which results in expedited growth. The outcome of this accelerated growth has caused the conversations of many leaders to shift to phrases such as: "We are running about 3500 now and God is continuing to take us to new levels." "We have grown to 1500 people in just two years." "We have added five additional services just to accommodate the growth." "How many are you running Doc?" These are all common phrases that now inundate the conversations among pastors and leaders of the church today. All too often it seems as if, they judge each other's success and relational worthiness based on the number of people that they run (almost as if God's people are a herd of animals). Without even realizing it, many of them have shifted their focus from maturing/transforming the minds of those to whom they minister, to rather maintaining the momentum of their ministries. It is this distorted focus that has given birth to a strategy that leads to deception, immorality, greed, pride, lack of integrity, lack of accountability, and more importantly has caused church leadership to operate outside of God's intended leadership strategy for the church/ the Body of Christ. Regaining our focus on humility and obedience to bring God's people to the place of maturity, transformation and ultimately discipleship is not just some concept or ideology. It is a necessity if we are to ever fulfill the great commission of making disciples of all nations (Matthew 28:19-20) and fully experience God's will for His Body (the church) here in the earth.

Paul declares the need for God's people to reach the level of maturity in the book of Ephesians Chapter 4 beginning at the latter of verses 13-15.

> That we may "measure up to the full stature of
> Christus.[14]Then we will no longer be like children,

*forever changing our minds about what we believe*

*because someone has told us something different*

*or because someone has cleverly lied to us and*

*made the lie sound like the truth. [15]Instead, we will*

*hold to the truth in love, becoming more and more*

*in every way like Christ, who is the head of his*

*body, the church."*

The latter verse in the original KJV translation says it this way,

*"..we may grow up into Him in all things, which is*

*the head, even Christ."* [2]

In the above passage, Paul not only expressed the need to bring God's people to maturity (which represents ***what*** we must do) and the outcome (***why*** we must do it) of maturing God's people, he also outlined the ***how*** we are to get it done. Paul outlined the very strategy that we are to use if we are to ever see it accomplished. Verse 11 states,

*"It was he who gave some to be apostles, some to be prophets, some to be evangelists, and some to be pastors and teachers, [12] to prepare God's people for works of service, so that the body of Christ may be built up [13] until we all reach unity in the faith and in the knowledge of the Son of God and become mature, attaining to the whole measure of the fullness of Christ."* [3]

Is it possible that the reason for the church's ineffectiveness at discipleship all points back to our (leadership) current church structure?  Is it possible that the people of God are not reaching a place of maturity, transformation, and discipleship because we have operated outside of the strategy designed by God to accomplish this (Doing God's Will, God's Way)? God's people must be brought to the place of maturity in their relationship with Christ in order that character will be built, believers will be equipped, and the Body of Christ will come to the unity of the faith and positioned to grow up and receive the fullness of God's intended purpose for the church (His Body).  It is with this conviction of heart and this end in mind, that I pursue **Discipleship or Deception** that will take us from ***where we are***, ***expound on how we got here***, *and emphasize* ***where we must go.***

# Introduction

One would expect conflict, dissension, discord, immorality, power struggles, lack of character/integrity, manipulation, selfishness, jealousy, envy, malice, confused perceptions, distorted beliefs/doctrines, bickering, and complaining to all be characteristics of individuals who are young, immature, and not yet developed through the process of life where circumstances are usually designed to birth maturity as we venture through our growth cycle. However, when these individuals have been processed through that cycle but somehow continue to possess these same characteristics, they have now become immature, and ineffective adults; who rather than being developed and matured enough to become examples whereby others may be trained, instead have become those who must continually be nurtured and cared for as mere children. How could such a thing happen and with who does the responsibility of this tragedy lie? As with any infant/child, whose minds are fertile ground waiting to be

1

molded and developed (built up) toward maturity, their dependency lies solely on those who have been entrusted to train and nurture them with the necessities of life that would bring them from the place of infancy to the place of maturity. Therefore, is it reasonable to place the blame on these individuals alone who have now become of age and must decide to continue being victims of improper guidance or to overcome by seeking alternative ways to grow up and reach the level of maturity? Or does the blame also rest with those who were entrusted with the care of these individuals but for whatever reason failed to provide the direction they needed to grow up and become mature adults that are prepared to train and impart wisdom to others?

As sad as it is, this analogy is not just a picture of bad parenting and/or immature adults; it is a reflection of the church today - its leaders and God's people-.

Consequently, we find that the majority of God's people are in this position spiritually and must ultimately assume full responsibility to overcome this dilemma by seeking out God's will for their own lives. Nonetheless, according to scripture the strategy of bringing God's people to the place of maturity rest upon those that are in leadership roles and have been entrusted with the care of God's children. Therefore, the accountability and responsibility for this constant breed of spiritually immature adults must also be assumed upon those who are in the leadership of the church.

In a world where we now have mega churches that accommodate thousands of people one would find it hard to believe that the church is ineffective at carrying out the mandate of discipleship. It would seem that the numbers alone would validate the success of the ministry. Unfortunately, it is to this standard that we have reduced our goals and objectives as leaders of God's people. In the practical world, if you produce many children and fail to raise them you are considered a dead beat. However, in the church consistent reproduction of immature children is not only applauded and accepted but apparently viewed with high esteem and admiration by many young emerging leaders whose goals are now just to lead large churches. Discipleship or Deception serves to bring consciousness to the reality of the condition of the church. It will briefly highlight the current state of the church in order to reawaken the awareness of its ineffectiveness and emphasize the necessity for transformation within the leadership of God's people. It will also highlight the cause and effects of how we got here in an effort to know what pitfalls and temptations we should avoid as we approach the shift to where God is taking us. Finally, it will express where we must go if we are ever to fulfill the Great Commission (Matthew 28:19-20) and offer an intentional strategy on how to proceed in getting there. If you grasp

4

the message of Discipleship or Deception, you will not only

rediscover the initial goal in leading God's people, but will

be equipped with God's strategy for fulfilling Jesus'

Commission to go and make disciples of all nations. It is

my prayer that all who would read this manuscript would

see the pattern of the church's ineffectiveness and realize

the necessity for a leadership shift in order to produce

mature saints to overcome it.

# *One*

## *Discipleship or Deception Exposed*

The greatest part of seeing God's plan come to past depends upon us doing ministry (God's Work), God's way. I cannot think of a better person to have modeled what true discipleship (making of disciples) is than the one who did it, was truly successful at it, and whose final command was that we go and do likewise. Unlike Jesus, most leaders today have sought out and emphasized the multitudes (numbers) of Jesus` ministry rather than the method (discipleship) he used to prepare for the multitudes. Most leaders assume that if they have many who follow and continue to support their ministries they must be doing the discipleship thing well. In fact, in a recent study on pastor's self-perception, "More than eight out of 10 pastors claim to be an "effective disciple-maker." [4] In the same article objectivity of the pastors' perceptions

6

were challenged by pointing out discrepancies between their self-view and reality based on other research. For instance, "The vast majorities of pastors describes their church as theologically conservative and effective at disciple-making, but still only a minority of churchgoers has actually developed a biblical worldview (live according to the Bible.)." [5]

Contradictions in what leaders are saying versus what is reflected in the church and the world seem to be very common in the western church today. Somehow we have allowed our minds to overlook the reality of the lack of progress being made as it relates to developing mature leaders for discipleship purposes. Statistics let us know that conversion growth in the American evangelical population has not taken place in the last 15-20 years. In fact, during this time there has been a 92% increase in those that are unchurched (up from 39 million to 75 million). [6] More research reveals that most unchurched adults were formerly churched, and that six out of ten unchurched people (62%) consider themselves to be Christian. [7] If that is not enough, a nationwide survey indicates as it relates to Holiness (living a consecrated life in right relationship with God), that "Holiness is a matter embraced by the Christian Church, but it is not one that many Americans adopt as a focal point of their faith development."[8]Simply stated it appears that those who are in the church today are a body of Christians who attend church and read the Bible.  However, they have no understanding of the concept or significance of holiness, have no personal desire to be holy, and therefore do very little (if anything) to pursue it.

So what does all of this mean?  It means that although 98% of pastors express great confidence in their capability as effective Bible teachers, 9 out of every 10 feel that they are effective leaders driven by a clear sense of vision, and 8 out of 10 claims to be effective disciple makers, the reality is that the church has still failed to:

- **reach** the lost,

- successfully **relate** to those who are or were once in the church,

- promote (**raise**) the central tenet of the Christian faith, 'Holiness,'

all of which Jesus' example of effective discipleship entailed. If we look closely at His ministry we will learn that His process for making disciples was a *multi-step process:*

- He first *reached* the lost (unchurched) by recruiting twelve men (not the multitude) not from those who represented leadership in the church of that time but from those who were in the world.

- He *related* to them by building relationships with them on a daily basis.

- He *raised* them by modeling, teaching, and training them to do the work of the Father.

9

- He empowered and *released* them to now go and do likewise with others (much of which we will discuss in later chapters).

His model served/serves as a clear and perfect example of how to do God's work, God's way.

Unless we experience a reality check and denounce the deception of judging our success "by nickels (the amount of money we raise), and noses" [9] (the number of people we "run" within our churches), we will never fulfill God's plan of discipleship nor experience the fullness of His power within the church when we submit in humility and obedience to doing God's Work God's Way.

# *T w o*

## *Two Extremes with no In Between*

What has been done? What have we accomplished? These are probably some of the questions that come to mind. The fact is rather than becoming effective at discipleship, we seemed to have ignored Paul's charge to endeavor to keep the unity of the Spirit [10] and instead have produced at least two extremes in the American church today. We have the church whose focus leans very heavily on the Spiritual aspects of Christ or we have the church whose focus leans very heavily on the Relational aspect of Christ.

A close examination of the distinctions between the two reveals that: the spiritually focused church leadership tends to emphasize spiritual gifts (speaking in tongues, prophecy, gifts of healing, deliverance gifts, etc.). They also have the ability to teach foundational truth but

11

sometimes lack relational skills and the ability to be relevant in their presentation. They often lead from afar and tend to assume that everyone has reached their level of Spiritual maturity in their relationship with Jesus. There is a heavy reliance on a variety of programs (Discipleship training, Bible Study groups, counseling groups, etc.) in an effort to bring about transformation in the lives of God's people. Their audience reflects believers who due to the absence of intimacy in their relationship with Christ, are captivated by the supernatural to stimulate encounters that suggests relationship. They have developed a dependency on people who have gotten close to God in order to substitute not being close to God themselves. Despite this church's ineffective and unproductive processes for discipleship, leadership is convinced of their position and unmoved by anyone or anything that suggests any other approach. While they possess great teaching ability and even understand the necessity of Spiritual gifts, their approach to discipleship lacks the ability to **reach** and **relate** to the unchurched; and/ or to **raise** those who are already in the church.

In contrast, the relationally focused church leadership tends to emphasize a very practical approach to disciple God's people. They present the gospel in relevant terms but oppose/suppress the supernatural in an effort to attract the seeker (unchurched). Leadership spends a great amount of time and money on conferences that informs them on the "to do's and not to do's" in leadership within the church with minimal emphasis on the Spiritual. Leadership has taken on more of the textbook approach to leading God's people. Their churches are inviting and have chosen the small group approach to intimacy and relationships in an effort to bring about transformation in the lives of God's people. These churches tend to grow rapidly because they have tapped into the importance of being relevant in today's society. Their audience reflects

13

more of the professional intellectual, leading edge technological crowd of believers than their counterpart. However, individuals in this church tend to lack a biblical worldview as it relates to their everyday life. Although this church is very relational in their approach toward the unchurched, they have neglected to (or chosen not to) develop strategies that will teach and challenge the people to desire deeper levels in their spiritual walk with Christ. As a result, the people have developed a misconception of holiness and have no urgent desire to grow in their faith and relationship with God.     Despite this church's ineffective and unproductive processes for discipleship, leadership is convinced of their position to reach the unchurched even though the Authority of the gospel is lacking and no real transformation is taking place in the lives of their people. While they possess great *relational* skills and may be better positioned to **reach** the lost, their approach to discipleship lacks the ability to **raise** *(teach)*

14

the un-churched to move beyond immaturity into a mature relationship with Christ.

So what has been accomplished? In the spiritually focused church we have failed to realize that discipleship only happens within relational environments. Somehow, we have overlooked that this was God's idea even from the beginning of time. After God created man and blessed him, His first command to him was to be fruitful and multiply (reproduce after your own kind). [11] Reproduction requires intimacy and intimacy only takes place in relationships. Jesus later comes along and confirms this fact with His last command to his disciples, "Go therefore and make disciples "[12] (reproduce). Because of the lack of relationships and relevancy, our spiritually focused churches have been diminished to platforms of sheer entertainment to accommodate the demands of the people who have predicated their entire walk with Christ based on seeing the supernatural rather than experiencing an intimate relationship with Christ. Leaders within these churches are compelled to entertain and perform in order to maintain momentum within their people. In the relationally focused church we have failed to realize that discipleship requires that we go beyond the practical/natural understanding and ability of man. We have not emphasized that there is no relationship with God without the Spirit of God [13] and that faith only works in the Spiritual. In an effort to be relevant and relational, we have suppressed the Authority of the gospel and have created environments that miscommunicate the results of a changed life. Due to the demands of the people who base their entire walk with Christ on practical knowledge while avoiding intimacy with the Spirit. Leaders in the relationally focused churches continue to adopt the thematic and motivational speaking approach in order to maintain momentum among their people.

Both extremes have managed to maintain a mass of believers, despite their contrasting focuses. In fact, most of the mega churches that exist today reflect the extreme of one or the other. Nevertheless, the fact still remains that in contrast to Jesus' success at His multi-step process of discipleship; the church today has failed to *reach* the unchurched, has been unsuccessful at *relating* to those who are or were in the church, and has failed to *raise* God's people to the place of maturity and discipleship. As a result, we have no hope of *releasing* God's people which is the last and most important aspect of discipleship if we are to be obedient to Jesus' command to "go". A mentor and friend once told me, "A circus can draw a crowd. However, big crowds do not mean that God thinks you are a success. What happens in the crowd is the miracle. Transformed lives are God's measurement of success."[14] Rather than minimizing our church focus to being Spiritual or Relational, we must again follow Jesus' example.    We must "master the merge" of the two extremes, and develop the in between, by becoming transformational in our focus so we will be transformational in our world; the true benefit of humility and obedience to doing God's Work God's Way.

# *T h r ee*

## *Cause and Effects*

Someone once said, "A road map and plan does you no good, unless you know where you are." [15] I believe the conclusion to that statement is "Ignorance of the routes we take is a definite plan for repeating the same mistakes." Hopefully by now you are asking, "How did this all happen? How did the church get to this place? There are many presuppositions as to the possible cause(s) of the church's ineffectiveness in making disciples today. However, our best conclusions should be derived from the ministry and life of Jesus. After all, the very purpose for which the church now exists (to make disciples) was first modeled and completed by Him. He was the first to accomplish this mighty task with impacting success. Thus insight into the oppositions of His ministry could also bring insight to the opposition of the church's ministry throughout the earth

19

today.  This could prove to be our only hope in restoring God's original purpose for the church.  It is easy for us to sometimes ignore the fact that Jesus did not complete His work of discipleship without opposition.  Although He was God in the flesh, we must be mindful that He was also a man in ministry.

> *We all know that Jesus came to help the descendants of Abraham, not to help the angels. Therefore, it was necessary for Jesus to be in every respect like us, his brothers and sisters, so that he could be our merciful and faithful High Priest before God. He then could offer a sacrifice that would take away the sins of the people. Since he himself has gone through suffering and temptation, he is able to help us when we are being tempted.*          ---Hebrews 2: 16- 18 NLT

If Christ was opposed as He carried out His ministry of making disciples in the earth, should we expect anything less than to encounter opposition as well? Scripture lets us know that despite clear evidence that Jesus was God and represented His new order in the earth, Jesus constantly faced opposition. Ironically, his opposition was not from those in the world, but from the Pharisees, Sadducees, and teachers of the law. [16] Leaders who claimed to represent God in the earth who were not only unsuccessful at doing so but somehow failed to recognize the very One that they said they were representing. Because we know Satan to be the enemy of God, it is common for us to expect opposition to God's purposes to come through him. However, when Satan uses our leaders to bring this opposition, we find it difficult to believe and even more difficult to accept or contend with. In Matthew 16:5 Jesus was aware of those who opposed him and His purpose. Therefore, He warns His disciples to guard against the ineffective teachings of the known leaders and teachers of the law of His time.

*"Watch out!" Jesus warned them. "Beware of the yeast of the Pharisees and Sadducees.....* Then at last they understood that he wasn't speaking about yeast or bread but about the false teaching of the Pharisees and Sadducees." [17]

---Matthew 16: 5b ....12

Throughout His ministry, Jesus continued to contend with, but overcome opposition from the religious leaders. Finally He decided to confront them by reversing their tactics and questioning these brilliant scholars regarding the Messiah. Matthew chapter 22 verses 41-46 reads,

*Then, surrounded by the Pharisees, Jesus asked them a question: "What do you*

*think about the Messiah? Whose son is he?" They replied, "He is the son of*

*David." Jesus responded, "Then why does David, speaking under the inspiration of the Holy Spirit, call him Lord? For David said, "The Lord said to my Lord, Sit in honor at my right hand until I humble your enemies beneath your feet." Since David called him Lord, how can he be his son at the same time?" No one could answer him. And after that, no one dared to ask him any more questions.* [18]

Though the Son of David did apply to Jesus, it was an inadequate description of the role of the Messiah. Even David recognized the Messiah as the Son of God and the Lord of everything. However, these men who were the leaders and teachers of the law in Jesus' day not only failed to recognize Him but they knew absolutely nothing about the Messiah's purpose (role) in the earth.

The current condition of the church implies that we are still faced with the same opposition and moreover the same "opposers" that Christ faced in His ministry of discipleship. The opposition represents any hindrance(s) to God's plan (making disciples). The opposers are still those who claim to represent God but continue to promote environments that produce ineffectiveness, immaturity, and therefore the un-fulfillment of the Great Commission to go and make disciples. Interestingly enough, up to this point in scripture Jesus had only warned His disciples against the Pharisees, Sadducees and teachers of the law. However, after the revealing fact that those who were viewed as representatives of God in the earth knew absolutely nothing about "God in the earth (Messiah's role in the earth)", He found it paramount enough to devote an entire chapter to clarify to the crowd and His disciples the reasons behind His warnings against these religious men. In essence, Jesus exposes and reveals a clear picture of the root cause of ineffective leadership. Matthew chapter 23 verse 2 begins,

*"The scribes and the Pharisees sit in Moses'*

*seat. [3]Therefore whatever they tell you to observe*

*that observe and do, but do not do according to*

*their works; for they say, and do not do."[19]*

In this passage Jesus' is saying, "These leaders who are

teachers of God's Word sit in the seats as ones who have

been with God. So what they are teaching is good and

worthy of obeying. However, do not be like them or do

what they do." What could possibly have warranted such

a statement from Jesus? One would think that those who

are teaching the Word of God would definitely model lives

worthy of emulation. As we look closer at the details of

Jesus' admonition, we will discover the liable "cause" to

their ineffective leadership.

*For they bind heavy burdens, hard to bear, and*

*lay them on men's shoulders; but they themselves*

*will not move them with one of their fingers. But all*

*their works they do to be seen by men. They make*

*their phylacteries broad and enlarge the borders of their garments. They love the best places at feasts, the best seats in the synagogues, greetings in the marketplaces, and to be called by men, 'Rabbi, Rabbi'.*[20]                    *--- Matthew 23:4-7 NKJV*

It is common practice for most leaders today to immediately excuse and exempt themselves from such practices as listed in this passage. Nevertheless, in our search for answers to the proven ineffectiveness of the church, it is worth an in depth look at the essence of the passages to see what may be revealed about those who are in leadership of God's people. From the many things that the Pharisees and teachers of the law were doing to warrant Jesus' rebuke, we can discover one common basis - each promoted "Superiority" rather than Servanthood. The leaders of that day had established a system that fostered "separation" between the people and themselves.

Jesus knew that their system was totally contrary to His ministry in the earth and consequently the ministry of His disciples so he not only exposed their issues but also gave stern and specific instructions to the disciples on how to avoid becoming like them.

> *Don't ever let anyone call you 'rabbi,' for you have only one teacher, and all of you are on the same I level as brothers and sisters. And don't address anyone here on earth as 'Father,' for only God in heaven is your spiritual Father. And don't let anyone call you 'Master,' for there is only one master, the Messiah. The greatest among you must be a servant.*[21]                    ---Matthew 23:8-11 NLT

The Greek word for rabbi is "rhabbi" which means an official title of honor. To avoid becoming like the religious leaders of His day, Jesus specifically instructed His disciples to denounce titles and to not allow anyone to address them in this manner. It is noteworthy to see that rather than mull over what the Pharisees were doing, He chose rather to emphasize the foundation of how and why they were able to do it.  They allowed their knowledge of God's Word to push them beyond service to the people and instead into a place of superiority over the people. Jesus knew that the greatest opposition to unity and the cause for division would come through the natural selfish desire to be superior even among His own people.  In a culture that determines ones level of significance by their titles and positions, it is quite easy to see how difficult it would be to avoid succumbing to the desires of superiority even in the church both then and now.  While the church does require structure and Godly order, it is not meant to be like an army with a clearly ranked chain of command that promotes superiority and inferiority.  Jesus clearly points out in verse 8 that we have only one Master who is Christ and that we are all brethren.  This makes it imperative that leaders in the church renounce all exalted

titles/positions and understand that the church is a
brotherhood of equals under Christ.  Status in the kingdom
is not to be determined by titles, but humility and
obedience to God's Will is the top priority for Christian
servant leaders.  In the American church, we have
rationalized and accepted titles as necessary in the name
of order.  And much like the leaders of Jesus' day, we have
promoted a system that creates "separation" between the
leaders and those who are being led.

## Effects on the People

### Isolation Impact

In Ephesians 4:13, Paul points out that one of the
prerequisites to becoming mature is "unity" in our faith.

> [13]*until we come to such unity in our faith and
> knowledge of God's Son that we will be mature and
> full grown in the Lord, measuring up to the full
> stature of Christ.*[22]

The impact of a system such as that of the Pharisees (superiority) not only defies unity but its effects in the church are deeper than what may be expected. Anytime there is superiority, there must be its direct opposite "inferiority". Inferiority means to be less than, substandard, and mediocre all of which breeds insecurity, fear, and isolation within those who find themselves in this position. Within our churches we have developed levels of people and created environments that are stifling to the growth and maturity of God's people. Most of our leaders have confused and replaced servant leadership with superior attitudes. Some of our church leaders have designated their own personal servants to carry their bibles, wipe the sweat from their faces, and attend to their every need. They justify these actions by labeling their attendants "armor bearers." While armor bearers are certainly biblical in nature, somehow we have managed to shift their purpose from being one who stands with and holds up the arms of the leader in battle into one who carries bibles and serves their every personal need.  Instead of servanthood being demonstrated by leaders who serve others, it is learned through others who serve leader(s) and those who may be in positions that appear to be superior.  While it is certainly honorable for those who follow to love and respect their leaders to the point of wanting to attend to their needs, it is crucial that leaders consider the extent of their servitude and the potential miscommunication of God's original intent.

*So after he had washed their feet, and had taken his garments, and was set down again, he said unto them, Know ye what I have done to you? Ye call me Master and Lord: and ye say well; for so I am. If I then, your Lord and Master, have washed your feet; ye also ought to wash one another's feet. For I have given you an example, that ye should do as I have done to you. Verily,*

*verily, I say unto you, the servant is not greater*

*than his lord; neither he that is sent greater than he*

*that sent him.*                         *---John 13:12-16 KJV*

Some leaders have now felt the need to implement body

guards who surround them and provide protection during

services. While it is a fact that times have changed and

church crimes are becoming more prevalent, it is

imperative to point out (without indicating any justification

for these crimes) that the root cause of many of these

crimes are partly related to the individual's feelings of

inferiority and insignificance. This system that is in place

has made it almost impossible for God's original design for

the church to be operable. Superiority breeds pride; pride

has caused those in these positions to create their own

kingdoms that they are not willing to give up. Rather than

creating an atmosphere where those who sit in the pews

week after week can grow and mature, they have caused

the majority of the people to feel that a certain level of

status must be attained in order for them to be anything or anybody that God can use.

**Unchallenged Relationships creates Unfulfilled Lives**

In most churches (large or small), it is normally the same group of individuals doing the work and/or being involved in the work of the ministry. This percentage is normally around 10 – 15%. Unfortunately, the majority of those that sit in the pews are faced with intimidation and gripped by fear that is a direct result of a system of superiority and isolation. The bible says, "Where the Spirit of the Lord is, there is liberty."[23] However, rather than promoting liberty most of our churches have become places of bondage for those who are victims of inferiority. Many leaders today wonder why they cannot seem to get more people to be involved in the work of the church. Never realizing that the very system (whether intentionally or unintentionally) created by them is the direct cause of the effect that they are now experiencing within their church. In his book entitled "Apostolic Government in the 21st Century", author Glenn Shaffer states, "Our church leaders are often discouraged because of the lack of ministry involvement of their members. They do not realize that the members have been excluded by the very order in which they operate."[24] Although many continue to come to church, their lack of involvement creates a lack of motivation for growth and thereby a lack of maturity in their relationship with God. It is a proven fact that anytime people are involved they feel a sense of ownership and a greater commitment. They feel a sense of significance that encourages them to challenge themselves to go beyond where they are and to excel at whatever it is that they are called to do. On the other hand, when there is no involvement, people are positioned to remain uncertain, unchallenged, unenthusiastic, and uninterested in moving beyond where they are currently.

As a result, most never realize their God given purpose nor pursue the fulfillment of the greatness that is locked inside of them.  They have resolved to be content in marveling at their leaders and assume that they are the only ones who can really get close to God.  The level of dependency on leaders has become so great that some do not even know how to pray for themselves or that they are permitted to pray.  Many have become personality driven and solely dependent on their leaders for the totality of their relationship with God.  This is why when a leader falls many people are devastated and sometimes unable to move beyond the pain of such a situation and to develop or continue to pursue of a relationship with God.  They depend on leaders to ultimately provide for them what they can really only receive from God.  However, instead of developing a personal relationship with God themselves, they spend their lives seeking out those whom they perceive as being close to God.  Just as the people of

Israel in the days of Samuel sought out and desired a king rather than God to rule over them[25], so is the desire of most of God's people today.

> *Finally, the leaders of Israel met at Ramah to*
> *discuss the matter with Samuel. "Look," they told*
> *him, "you are now old, and your sons are*
>
> *not like you. Give us a king like all the other nations*
> *have." Samuel was very upset with their request*
> *and went to the LORD for advice. "Do as they say,"*
> *the LORD replied, "for it is me they are rejecting,*
> *not you. They don't want me to be their king any*
> *longer.*
>
> *------ I Samuel 8:4-7*

When dependency on our leaders extends beyond honor and healthy submission to authority, it is a true representation of a desire to have our leaders rule over us and therefore causes us to reject God and deny Him as our King.

In his book "The Pursuit of Purpose" Dr. Miles Monroe states, "The deepest craving of the human spirit is to find a sense of significance and relevance"[26] without a relationship with our Creator, it is impossible for us to know what we were created to do. Masses of people, even in our churches, are searching for relevance and significance. They exist in this world and continue to ask themselves, "What on earth am I here for?" They are ignorant of their purpose because they are disconnected from the source of that purpose. One of the reasons "The Purpose Driven Life"[27], authored by Rick Warren has become such a sought after resource is because it was an awakening to many people that they are not insignificant. Despite the systems of this world including the system in our churches, people began to realize that they were created with purpose. This resource stirred something deep down inside of the masses that had been buried by the systems of superiority and suppression. Some were changed and some were set free. Unfortunately, due to the inability of our current church structures to sustain such a life giving/transforming message for many it became just another temporary resource of inspiration and motivation. Dr. Monroe states, "Your fulfillment in life is dependent on your being and doing what you were born to be and do." [28] Many have gone to their graves without ever realizing let alone fulfilling their purpose in life. Many more though living, have yet to discover true fulfillment in life. Jeremiah 1:5 says, *"Before I formed thee in the belly I knew thee; and before thou camest forth out of the womb I sanctified thee.*[29] True fulfillment in life is solely dependent upon discovering the Creator's purpose and plan for our lives. The plan and purpose can only be revealed by the One who designed it and thus designed us for it. Outside of relationship with the Creator, purpose will never be realized. And life without realization of purpose is a greater tragedy than death itself. Dr. Monroe expresses it this way, "The greatest tragedy in life is not death, but life without a reason."[30] The critical effect of systems of superiority is that they not only create dependency and breed immaturity, but ultimately they produce death.

## Effects on the Leaders

### Lack of Accountability

In reference to Jesus' instructions to his disciples in Matthew 23:8 to not allow anyone to address them by titles, I have heard many of today's leaders express that this only applied to the Pharisees because they were abusing their authority and their positions. While this is definitely the context which prompted Jesus to speak on this matter, His emphasis in verse 8 shifts to instructing his disciples in what they should do in contrast to what was being done by the Pharisees. "Don't ever let anyone call you 'rabbi,' for you have only one teacher, and all of you are on the same level as brothers and sisters."[31] His instructions are a continuation from verse 3 when He states plainly for them to do what they say but do not do what they do.[32]

> *So practice and obey whatever they say to you, but don't follow their example.*     ---Matthew 23:3 NLT.

Notice, Jesus never said as long as you do not abuse your authority it is permissible to be referred to by titles. In fact, in the latter part of verse 8 Jesus also opposes the use of titles by placing emphasis on and explicitly stating that His disciples were/are on the same level as brothers and sisters. The same level definitely indicates equality and condemns superiority. Earlier when the disciples disputed over who was the greatest among them, Jesus expressed to them that in order to be first, they must be last and servant of all.[33] It is in this moment of instruction that Jesus reiterates the same statement as he expressed to them on the issue of referring to each other with titles.

> *But he who is greatest among you shall be your servant.* --Matthew 23:11 NKJV.

Unlike brothers and sisters who are equal in all aspects, leaders who operate on the basis of titles are already in opposition to Jesus' model for His disciples. Many leaders would argue that their uses of titles are only a form of order used to distinguish whose leading however, they still promote equality among everyone in their church. We would have to ask is it possible to use titles which are designed to separate the leaders from the followers and truly say that we promote equality. Better yet, is it possible to use titles and not eventually walk in the same pride, selfishness, and superiority as that of the Pharisees? In a society and culture that is conditioned and controlled by a system of titles and positions, it is fundamentally impossible to implement such a system in God's church but separate the baggage that it promotes. In our corporate world, titles and positions are sought out because they dictate status, power, supremacy, and most importantly level of compensation. Titles in our churches do not change the motivation that drives them. It is no different than that of our world. They do not just symbolize order within our churches; they dictate status, power, supremacy, and level of compensation.

- It is this status and power that permits limited accountability among our leaders.

- It is this status and power that allows our leaders to fail morally and continue to lead God's people as if nothing has ever happened.

- It is this status and power that allow leaders to manipulate God's Word to justify the ordaining of homosexual Bishops to provide Godly leadership to God's people.

- It is this status and power that enable leaders to influence their followers to participate in cultic religions.

- It is this status and power that is responsible for the lack of integrity and morality displayed by some of our leaders today.

- It is this status and power that causes leaders to covet associations with popular leaders and continue to propagate the superiority systems within our churches.

- It is this same status and power that causes leaders to create environments of dependency rather than environments of maturity and growth.

A journalist for a Christian magazine points out exactly how far astray status and power in our churches can go. In an article entitled, "It's Getting Really Weird Out There" the author writes, "At one charismatic mega church staff pastors successfully convinced all their wives and female staff members to get breast implants. A church in California (known for its revival meetings and prophetic ministry) imploded after members learned that several men in the church had been having homosexual affairs with the pastor, who was married. A leader with an international following (who wears the label of "apostle") informed his leaders that men of God who reach his level of anointing are allowed to have more than one sexual partner. Then his own son offered his wife to his father out of a sense of spiritual obligation." [34] It is only through systems of superiority initiated by titles which produce status, positions, and power that such drastic situations are able to infiltrate our churches.

Status and position also create popularity and/or fame. When we think of those who are famous, we immediately think of those who are highly esteemed by the world and classified as stars. These usually include: movie stars, recording artists, professional athletes, and others. The most common quality shared by most of these people is that they usually do not associate much with ordinary people. They do not invite "common" individuals into their homes and their guest list to events does not include the average "joe". Totally contrary to any characteristic Jesus taught or modeled. However, the quest for fame and popularity has somehow made its way into the objectives of some of our leaders in the church today. While surfing the web for music from a well-known worship leader, I was disappointed to read a news article that stated that this artist had to postpone his appearance to thousands in an un-reached country due to being nominated for four Grammy Awards and having to be present at the awards. Because of my love of this artist, I want to believe that his decision to postpone his appearance for ministry to the lost and unreached is for ministry opportunities to others who are lost at the Grammy Awards. Many times we justify our own desires by statements such as, "we must go among sinners and minister just as Jesus did". While this is definitely a true statement, it is imperative that we note that when Jesus did go among sinners His purpose was not only pure but effective. There was no leaven in the bread that He served. Therefore, His impact resulted in conversions for the kingdom of God rather than invitations to party with those who appear superior. Along with popularity and fame usually comes the greatest benefit of systems of superiority, "compensation". "For the love of money people will rob their own mother" are lyrics to the very popular song "For the Love of Money". Unfortunately, this statement has come to now accurately describe some of the leadership in our churches. Titles and positions not only open the door to a lack of accountability with church finances, but also positions leaders to use their influence to manipulate God's people to give their money to accomplish their own personal agendas. This usually results in the leaders continuing to profit while the people continue to be deprived. In I Timothy 6 Paul declares to Timothy,

*"True religion with contentment is great*

*wealth. After all, we didn't bring anything with us*

*when we came into the world, and we certainly*

*cannot carry anything with us when we die. So if we*

*have enough food and clothing, let us be*

*content. But people who long to be rich fall into*

*temptation and are trapped by many foolish and*

*harmful desires that plunge them into ruin and*

*destruction. For the love of money is at the root of*

*all kinds of evil. And some people, craving money,*

*have wandered from the faith and pierced*

*themselves with many sorrows."*[35]

*--- I Timothy 6:6-10 NLT*

Money is necessary in order to finance the ministry of the

gospel. However, the love of it has produced many

sorrows some for the leaders, but mostly for those who

follow. Through systems of superiority some of our leaders

preach a prosperity gospel that makes empty promises to

God's people through manipulation of God's word. Just as the Pharisees did through religious demands, today's leaders place these burdens upon the shoulders of God's people while they themselves are not affected by it. Compensation has also caused many leaders to compromise truth. In our spiritually focused churches, where we place emphasis on the supernatural, leaders have a tendency to somehow always relate the supernatural blessings of God back to money. Though there are times when God does challenge us through stewardship (which is not just our treasure but our time and talent), some leaders take advantage of this environment where God's people are vulnerable to make promises that never manifest in their lives based on the amount of money that they give. Unfortunately, because most of God's people are vulnerable, dependent, and immature they give out of obligation and guilt and usually end up more damaged in the process. In the relational focused churches, some leaders deliberately choose the unchallenging motivational approach of leadership in fear of losing individuals who are prominent givers. Their people give out of status and control and are still damaged due to miscommunication of stewardship.

**Lack of Integrity**

Positions, status, supremacy, and levels of compensation bring great affluence and influence. Unfortunately, affluence has created a lack of integrity in some of our church leadership today. Some leaders' response to the people is based on their level of affluence. I visited this mega-church in a very prominent and affluent area of Frisco, Texas. I had visited this church a few times and was impressed at their emphasis on being relational. I was even utilizing their kid's summer camp for my children. Because my wife and I were in the process of starting a ministry in this area, one evening I decided that I would try and schedule an appointment with the pastor of this church just to introduce myself and become acquainted. I

proceeded to the reception area and began to inquire of

their process for meeting the pastor. The young lady at the

desk immediately responded (without even thinking about

it) "oh, our pastor doesn't meet with people". After the

startled look on my face, she began to fumble over her

words to try and make up for what had just come out of her

mouth. I then introduced myself as an emerging leader in

the area and explained that my effort was simply to

become acquainted with other leaders in the area. Her

response was, "Oh, so you're a pastor? I'm sorry. I didn't

know. I will have someone from his office contact you, if

you would leave me a number." I left there that day asking

myself, "How is it that leaders express being relational, but

have positioned themselves to never relate to ordinary

people?" Even though her response in person was

different when she learned that I was an emerging leader

in the area, I still never received a phone call from anyone at that church. This seems to have become the norm for a great number of our church leaders today. The integrity to communicate with ordinary people has been lost. Much like the Pharisees of Jesus' day, many of our leaders preach things that they themselves are not willing to live up to.[36]

## Burnout –positioned for failure

Systems of superiority can also be blamed for the unconscious effect of leadership burnout. It is referred to as unconscious because it is one that is not easily recognizable as being a result of systems of superiority. Many of today's leaders are experiencing leadership burnout and have never considered that the cause of it could be related to their current leadership structure. As confusing as it may sound, burnout is the "cause and effect" of the "cause and effect". As a result of the isolation impact (inferiority /superiority factor that was discussed earlier in this chapter) and the effect it has had on the people, leaders are now faced with the sole responsibility of providing all of the leadership themselves or by dictating rather than delegating to other individuals that will only serve as an extension of their own efforts. This leaves little room for creative input from others which in turn limits the vision to effectively lead God's people. This has created stressful environments where leaders must sustain the superhero approach to ministry in order to maintain momentum among the people within their congregations. In an effort to stay afloat leaders implement strategies (emphasize spiritual gifts - Spiritually focused church, emphasize relationships- Relationally focused church) that will continue to draw the people but has lost the ability to retain and lead them into true discipleship (see Chapter 2 – Two Extremes with No In Between). Because some leaders are very gifted and more broadly skilled than others, the ineffectiveness of the superhero approach sometimes takes longer to manifest; thereby deceiving these leaders into believing that they are effective at discipleship (see Chapter 1 Discipleship or Deception). Despite what these leaders believe, we must face the fact. With no conversion growth in the church for the last twenty plus years; it is quite plain to see that our church environments have promoted systems of superiority and as a result have had no other alternative but to shift from maturing God's people to maintaining momentum / motivation and are therefore positioned for ongoing failure to fulfilling the great commission of making disciples of all men.

# *Four*

## Strategy for Overcoming

### The Natural Approach

Now that we know where we are and how we got here, it is only fitting to address where we must go and the possible strategy of how to get there. In a world driven by status, rank, and class you are probably wondering how it is possible to operate without titles, positions, and systems of superiority. Because our western world is a democracy and this approach is common to our culture (government, education system, and corporate America) it has naturally become the way we have elected to structure leadership in our churches. Though this approach continues to prove successful and effective in our natural world, it is quite evident that it has not been effective in the church. We must realize and accept that the measurement of success in our natural world is not necessarily the measurement of success in the Spiritual world. While the goals and objectives in corporate America may be to increase the profit margins by 20%, or in education to obtain the highest level degree in a specialized field, or in government to someday become a distinguished and prominent elected official, we should effortlessly agree that our goals and objectives in the church are totally different from that of our world. If this is the case, it should also be obvious to us that our approach toward effective church leadership/structure should not be patterned after the world, but instead according to God's order and example.

**The Necessary Approach**

In his book, "Rediscovering the Kingdom", Dr. Miles Monroe does an excellent job in expounding on how important it is that we (those who follow Christ) realize that God's ultimate purpose for the church is to establish His Kingdom in the earth (the visible world), just as it has already been established in the heavens (the invisible world). He accomplished this by creating man in His image and giving him dominion over the earth (the Garden of Eden).[37] This represented a perfect Kingdom in the earth realm where then humanity and Divinity walked together in complete unity. Unfortunately when man fell, he not only lost access to the Kingdom, but the relationship that authorized him as a representative of the King in the earth. Every since the fall of man, God has sought to re-establish His Kingdom on earth and the relationship where He (Divinity) and His creation (humanity) can once again walk in complete unity. In order to regain the Kingdom, God introduced His own son into the human equation by the power of incarnation. Through Jesus' death, burial, and resurrection the Kingdom was once again regained. As a result, the authority to re-establish and represent the King on earth was and is now given through relationships with Jesus the King.

*All authority has been given to Me in heaven and*

*on earth.*   --Matthew 28:18 *NKJV*

Once again it became possible for humanity and Divinity to

walk together in complete unity. Before the King's

departure from the earth and ascent to the heavenly

realm, He provided our (the church) orders or in modern

terms our goals and objectives.

*Go therefore and make disciples of all the nations,*

*baptizing them in the name of the Father, and of the*

*Son and of the Holy Spirit teaching them to observe all*

*things that I have commanded you.*

-- Matthew 28:19 *NKJV*

As it is in the natural (corporate America), so it is in the

Spiritual (the church). Success can only be declared as

we attain and fulfill our goals and objectives. However,

due to the vast difference between the goals of the church

and the goals in our world, the strategies used to pursue

our goals must also be vastly different. Jesus was the first to demonstrate success in making disciples throughout His earthly ministry, and the result was mature believers who were also effective at making disciples. Through the words of Paul he provided the structure that would enable us to be effective and successful at reaching our goal of making disciples. In Ephesians chapter 4, Paul begins by entreating us to first, walk worthy of what we have been called (ordered by the King) to do. Then he expounds on some of the character traits necessary to keep the unity of walking with the King.

> *I, therefore, the prisoner of the Lord, beseech you to walk worthy of the calling with which you were called, with all lowliness and gentleness, with longsuffering, bearing with one another in love, endeavoring to keep the unity of the Spirit in the bond of peace.*          ---Ephesians 4:1-3 *NKJV*

We must note that the traits that he listed: lowliness, gentleness, and longsuffering are all traits that are not common in environments that promote superiority.   In verse six, he declares that there is only one who is in charge and above (superior to) all.[38]

> One God and Father of all, who is above all...
>
>                                    ---Ephesians 4:6 *NKJV*

He then picks up where the King (Jesus) departed into the heavenly realm and enlightens us on what happened as He departed.   Paul emphasizes that when the King ascended into heaven, in His grace He gave gifts (not titles) unto men and in verse 11 he exclaims what those gifts were.

> *And He Himself gave some to be apostles, some prophets, some evangelists, and some pastors and teachers,*                    ---Ephesians 4:11 *NKJV*

Many leaders have manipulated God's Word as not declaring these as leadership gifts (Ephesians 4:11), but have naturally claimed them to be titles.  The very nature of our culture is mainly responsible for this.  However, it may help if we note the difference in a gift and a title. A gift is something that is freely given and usually readily received. It is therefore cherished. In this context it represents an ability, talent, or skill. Because a gift is something that is freely given, it is usually handled with care and more naturally shared with others. On the other hand, a title is something that is earned and though it too is cherished it signifies ownership and entitlement. Because it is earned, it is usually not shared with others but instead forced upon others as a measure of control and/or as a sign of superiority. God's intentions were never for any of us to control the other, but that each gift just as it has been freely given would also be given freely toward restoring God's people back to the place of walking in unity with the King.

> *for the equipping of the saints for the work of ministry, for the edifying of the body of Christ, till we all come to the unity of the faith and of the*

*knowledge of the Son of God, to a perfect man, to*

*the measure of the stature of the fullness of Christ;*

                    ---Ephesians 4:12-13 *NKJV*

This was the necessary strategy for bringing God's people

to the place of maturity, assuring that we attain to the

measure and the stature of the King in order to once again

effectively represent Him on the earth, and thereby

successfully obtain our goal and objective of making

disciples.

*that we should no longer be children, tossed to and*

*fro and carried about with every wind of doctrine, by*

*the trickery of men, in the cunning craftiness of*

*deceitful plotting, but speaking the truth in love,*

*may grow up in all things into Him who is the*

*head—Christ-*          ---Ephesians 4:14-15 *NKJV*

**Surely the Pastor is the Head!**

Partly due to the nature of our culture, our natural

inclination to titles (systems of superiority) has totally

misconstrued God's perfect strategy and caused the massive chaos that currently exists in most of our churches today. Because we have taken the strategies of our natural world and implemented them in our churches in place of God's Divine strategy we have become conditioned to believe that God has placed one man / woman in charge as the head of our local churches. Thus, we have created titles such as Pastor, Senior Pastor, Executive Senior Pastor, and many more. In doing so, not only have we eliminated a place for the other leadership gifts, but we have also destroyed the intended strategy of each leadership gift to freely work together in order to accomplish the King's order –God's Work-. We have ceased to rely on the King's strategy –God's way-, re-classified the gifts as titles and placed the control and responsibility into the hands of one individual (the pastor) who in our culture, is now referred to as the "head". In order to provide justification for this approach we have even created doctrines that teach that some of the other gifts, namely the Apostles and Prophets no longer exist in our world.

I remember taking a New Testament Survey class in Bible College where the professor, a world-renowned and well respected man of God, was teaching from a reference in the book of Acts. In his lecture on the Apostles he made the statement that, "there are no apostles or prophets of today, the only ministries that are operable are that of the evangelist, teacher, and the pastor." As he continued to teach, I found it difficult to follow, because I could not get past that statement. The cardinal rule of the class was *that we were there to learn and not to debate the scriptures*, so I longed for the upcoming break. It was at this point that I would ask the professor personally for a more definitive reason for his conclusion that there were no longer Apostles and Prophets in God's church. At the break, I proceeded to ask my question regarding the

63

cessation of the Apostolic and the Prophetic within the church. In a very defensive tone the professor asked me, "Are you trying to imply that you are an Apostle or a Prophet?" My reply was, "Sir, I just wanted clarity of your reasoning behind this statement. I was not implying that I am either. However, I believe that I should be whatever God wants me to be and if that's an Apostle or a Prophet, I'm very open to that as well." He proceeded to tell me that if I had not seen Jesus face to face; or planted churches; or performed signs, miracles and wonders there was no way that this was possible. Finally, he reminded me of the ***class rule*** - that scriptures in the class were not debatable.

In our resolve to combine our culture with God's church, we perpetuate doctrines that justify our systems of status, power, and superiority. Although God's plan never endorsed the single gift (let alone the title) of pastor as head (Ephesians 4:15) of the local church, we continue to maintain and organize our churches based on this system, which has proven time and time again to be ineffective.  In fact as we continue to study the strategy given by God through Paul, we learn that the only head in which the Body of Christ (the church) is to mature and grow up into, is Christ.  There was something in my heart that would not allow me to leave the situation with my instructor alone. After receiving godly counsel and reading through the book of Ephesians, I discovered that the answer to my question had already been addressed in God's strategy.  It was as if God's plan had already considered what leaders in our culture would do in order to validate their own desires and make sense of their views.  The answers were revealed right in the same passage in the common questions *who, when, what, why* and *how.*  According to Paul, we know *who* gave the leadership gifts (Jesus); we know *when* He gave them (as he ascended back to heaven); we know *what* he gave (gifts to men); we even know *why* he gave them (for the equipping of the saints for the work of ministry and for the edifying of the body); and if we continue to examine God's strategy, it also reveals *how* long (til we come to the unity of the faith and of the knowledge of the Son of God, to a perfect man, to the measure of the stature of the fullness of Christ). It is quite evident that the church is a long way from coming to the place of unity of the faith and definitely to the place of the knowledge of Jesus. Rick Joyner in his book, "The Apostolic Ministry" states, "We must realize that we still need all of these gifts/ministries in order to be the church that God have created us to be."[39] The Pastoral gift/ministry can never be what he is designed to be until the Apostolic, Prophetic, Evangelistic, and Teaching gifts/ministries are all operating and contributing to the plan. In obedience, I decided to share this with my instructor. I went back to school and pointed this out being very cautious not to offend him, only to be dismissed by the instructor with the class rule, "**we're not here to debate the scriptures.**"

**If not the Head, then What?**

We have already established that the difference in a gift and a title is that a gift is freely given while titles are earned and represent a form of control. Although the gifts that Jesus gave were leadership gifts, they were never meant to be considered as the head of the church. In our culture this can be difficult to comprehend, because we are conditioned to automatically associate anyone in leadership as being the head. This mentality has played a dominant role in the confusion in our current church structure. You may ask, "How is it possible to be in leadership and not be the head?" As stated earlier, Christ is the head of the church, both locally and globally. This is why the entire church (including leadership) is referred to as the Body of Christ. Our goal is to unite, mature into perfection, and grow up into the Head who is Christ which once again establishes His full presence in the earth and empowers us for effective discipleship. In order to accomplish this, Jesus gave each one of us gifts that all play a role in assuring the success of our goal. Ephesians 4:7 states," to each one of us grace was given according to the measure of Christ's gift." In other words, Christ Himself decided who would play which role in the Body, but placed equal significance on each role(grace was given to us all). Consider the natural body; it is made up of many parts some that play major roles (heart, brain, liver, etc.) in the way the body functions. However, for the body to be considered perfectly healthy even parts that may be considered minor (tonsils, kidneys, fingers, toes, etc.) must play their role and is therefore of equal significance. When God created the natural body, he created it in such a way that the major and minor parts are both dependent on each other in order to produce a perfectly healthy body. Just as it is with the natural body, so it is with the church (the Body of Christ). I Corinthians 12 say it this way,

> *For as the body is one and has many members, but all the members of that one body, being many, are one body, so also is Christ........*
>
> *For in fact the body is not one member but many.*
>
> *If the foot should say, "Because I am not a hand, I am not of the body," is it therefore not of the body? And if the ear should say, "Because I am not an eye, I am not of the body," is it therefore not of the body? If the whole body were an eye, where would be the hearing? If the whole were hearing, where would be the smelling? But now God has set the members, each one of them, in the body just as He pleased. And if they were all one member, where would the body be?*
>
> --- I Corinthians 12:12, 14-19 *NKJV*

Although the Apostle, Prophet, Evangelist, Pastor, and Teacher are given the leadership roles they are still considered to be members of the Body of Christ. Understanding this is vitally important in our warfare against systems of superiority and our natural tendency to conform to the leadership structures of our culture. This is also beneficial in helping God's people overcome inferiority complexes that have been created through isolation between leadership and the people. I Corinthians 12:20 says,

> *But now indeed there are many members, yet one body. And the eye cannot say to the hand, "I have no need of you"; nor again the head to the feet, "I have no need of you." No, much rather, those members of the body which seem to be weaker are necessary. And those members of the body which we think to be less honorable, on these*

*we bestow greater honor; and our un-presentable parts have greater modesty, but our presentable parts have no need. But God composed the body, having given greater honor to that part which lacks it, that there should be no schism in the body, but that the members should have the same care for one another. And if one member suffers, all the members suffer with it; or if one member is honored, all the members rejoice with it.*      *- I Corinthians 12:20-26 NJKV*

In environments that promote status, positions, titles, and superiority, **body ministry** will never take place. It is only when we recognize Christ as the Head; accept the gifts/roles that have been given to us by Christ's grace; walk as Paul stated in the beginning of Ephesians 4 "in a way that is worthy of what we have been called to"; and honor each gift/role with equal significance (God's work, God way) that we will begin to see the Body of Christ attain

71

our goal of reaching the place of unity, maturing into perfection, and growing up into Christ who is the Head.

**Surely there has to be order!**

Most of us have heard the very familiar statement, *"Anything with two or more heads is a monster"*. This is a very common response among leaders in our culture when a plurality of leadership is discussed as the form of church government. Although some leaders agree and can plainly see that God's order of leadership for the church is definitely inclusive of the *Five Gifts*, they have resolved to continue the common cultural approach to leadership due to its familiarity and non-confrontational nature. Other leaders continue to reject God's order due to their inability or unwillingness to relinquish control. To address the concerns of leaders who would still not be convinced that plurality of leadership is possible, God's strategy even *provided* the order in which the gifts were to function in the body.

*Now you are the body of Christ, and members individually. And God has appointed these in the church: first apostles, second prophets, third teachers, after that miracles, then gifts of healings, helps, administrations, varieties of tongues. Are all apostles? Are all prophets? Are all teachers? Are all workers of miracles? Do all have gifts of healings? Do all speak with tongues? Do all interpret? But earnestly desire the best gifts. And yet I show you a more excellent way.*

*---I Corinthians 12:27-31 NKJV*

This would also assure that each member of the body would learn to accept, appreciate, and celebrate the necessity for the diversity of gifts within the Body of Christ.

In an interview with Bishop Tony Miller of Destiny World Outreach I asked him to share his thoughts on possible ways that this necessary change in structure would take place. His response was as follows:

73

"Much of the change will come through the emerging churches/generations. In the Old Covenant, Saul represented the old order and David represented the new order. Two worlds existed at the same time. Saul lived in a Palace. David lived in a Tent. Jonathan recognized David for who he was and even accepted that his father was a hindrance to God's will. However, he still left David after telling him that his father meant him no good and went back and died in battle with his father. There is a generation of preachers that recognize the new order but will not overcome the security of the old and will return to die with their Daddys."[40]

It is my sincere prayer that leaders would no longer allow themselves to be deceived into believing that fulfillment of the Great Commission will be accomplished through our current church leadership structure. But rather, begin to see and accept that God's strategy is not only the best way, it is the only way in which we are guaranteed to be effective and successful at equipping God's people for the work of ministry, reaching the unity of the faith, maturing into perfection, measuring up to the full stature of Jesus, and thereby growing up into Him who is the Head – Christ our King.

# *F I v e*

## The Benefits of having them all

### Human Anatomy- 101

The human body is composed of a ten system group of tissues and organs that work together to perform well-defined functions. Each body system coordinates its' activities with those of other systems to maintain the healthy functioning of the entire body. Its' highly organized anatomy enables the human body to perform a wide variety of life-sustaining activities including fighting off infections, digesting nutrients, growing, and reproducing.[41] It is not ironic that the church is referred to as the Body of Christ but in fact, quite ingenious. I am always amazed at how God is so consistent and never contradicting in His plans and His purposes. In His ultimate pursuit of reconnecting humanity (His people) with Divinity (Himself), God has always used natural things in order to convey a spiritual message (i.e. the Tabernacle = Picture of Jesus, wheat and tares = righteous and unrighteous, etc.). Amazingly, He continues this model to simplify the divine order for His church. Just as the natural body (though composed of many different systems) must work together in order to perform well-defined functions, so it is with the Body of Christ.

> *The body is a unit, though it is made up of many parts; and though all its parts are many, they form one body. So it is with Christ.*
>
> *---I Corinthians 12:12 NKJV*

Within the systems of the natural body there are multiple functions that must be carried out and multiple parts of the body designed to fulfill those functions.   Figure 5.1 on the following page illustrates this point.

## 10 Systems of the Human Body

| Systems | Functions | Parts |
|---------|-----------|-------|
| Circulatory | uses blood to deliver oxygen and nutrients | Artery, Veins |
| Endocrine | release chemical substances into the bloodstream | Pancreas, Glands |
| Urinary | eliminates waste products from the body | Kidneys, Bladder |
| Human Skeleton | supports the body and protects internal organs | Bones, Cartilage |
| Nervous | oversees the activity of all other body systems | Brain, Spinal cord |
| Muscular | attach to bones and control all voluntary movements | Pectoralis, Biceps, Triceps |
| Respiratory | Provides oxygen to cells throughout the body and removes carbon dioxide from the body | Lungs, Nose |

| | | |
|---|---|---|
| | break down food into simpler substances | Liver, Intestines |
| **Digestive** | For absorption into the bloodstream | |
| | | |
| **Immune** | defends the body from invading organisms | Spleen, Lymph nodes |
| | | |
| **Reproductive** | male-form reproductive cells, and deliver them to the female | Penis, Scrotum |
| | | |
| | female-producing female sex cells also protects and nurtures a developing baby and provide nourishment for newborns | Vagina, Uterus, Breasts |
| | | |

**Figure 5.1**

When the natural body is unhealthy, it is usually the result of a certain body part failing to perform its' function(s) thereby causing the related system(s) to malfunction. Although the natural body may continue its' existence, in this condition it is prone to infections, lack of growth (immaturity), and lack of reproduction.  It is true that the natural body contains certain parts that may be removed and yet continues to function; however, it is noteworthy to mention that those parts of the body typically represent the defense and or regulatory mechanisms of the body.  For example, the thyroid gland in the endocrine system may be removed from the body; however, the hormones (chemicals that the gland would normally release into the bloodstream) would no longer be present to influence and regulate activities such as metabolism, growth, mental development, and emotional behavior.  In the immune system certain parts may also be removed from the body;

consequently, this subjects the body to invading organisms, disease, and foreign substances.

On the other hand, there are certain parts of the body, if failing to perform their function, will not only cause its' related system(s) to malfunction but would cause the entire body to malfunction. Under these circumstances, the body would cease all of life's activities and the end result is death. It is striking to note that these parts of the body inevitably are responsible for assuring that everything flows properly. For example, the coronary artery/heart in the circulatory system pumps blood to deliver oxygen and nutrients to body tissues. The lungs in the respiratory system provide oxygen to cells and remove carbon dioxide from the body. The brain and spinal cord in the nervous system provide oversight and connect with the rest of the body to control both voluntary and involuntary functions.

It is quite evident that each body system must coordinate its' function(s) with those of other systems in order to maintain a whole healthy functioning body.  The benefit of such unity within the human body is that it positions the body with the ability to perform life-sustaining activities such as: fighting off infections, digesting nutrients, growing, and reproducing.

**Christ-atomy 101**

If we accept the message being conveyed through Paul's analogy, we would understand that as it is with the human body, so it is with the Body of Christ.  The Body of Christ is comprised of many gifts which are empowered by nine body systems (fruits of the spirit: love, joy, peace, forbearance, kindness, goodness, faithfulness, gentleness and self-control) and one Head (Christ) that work together to perform well-defined functions (gifts).  Each body system coordinates its' activities with those of other systems to maintain the healthy functioning of the entire Body of Christ.  Its' highly organized anatomy enables the entire Body of Christ to perform a wide variety of life-sustaining activities including: fighting off the enemy, digesting the milk and meat of the Word, growing to maturity, and eventually reproducing (making disciples). Empowered through the systems of the Body of Christ (fruits of the Spirit) there are multiple functions (gifts) that must be carried out and multiple parts (members) of the body designed to fulfill those functions (gifts).

*For in fact the body is not one member but many.*

*---I Corinthians 12:14 NKJV*

*There are diversities of gifts, but the same Spirit. There are differences of ministries, but the same Lord. And there are diversities of activities, but it is the same God who works all in all.*

*---I Corinthians 12:4-6 NKJV*

For centuries, the Body of Christ has managed to continue its' existence without certain parts (members) performing their functions (gifts). The results have been disabling over the years and have caused the entire body to malfunction. Just as it is with the natural body, at this critical level the body could cease all of life's activities and the end result would be death. We must understand how imperative it is that all parts (members) of the body actively perform their functions, but we must begin by first reviving those parts that are designed to sustain life and are inevitably responsible for assuring that everything flows properly within the Body. As stated, in the natural body these represent the coronary artery/heart, the lungs, the brain and spinal cord, and so on. However, in the Body of Christ they represent the apostle, prophet, evangelist, pastor, and teacher.

> *And God has appointed these in the church: first apostles, second prophets, third teachers..........*
>
> *---I Corinthians 12:28a NKJV*
>
> *And He Himself gave some to be apostles, some prophets, some evangelists, and some pastors and teachers, for the equipping of the saints ...... that*

*we….. may grow up in all things into Him who is the head—Christ—from whom the whole body, joined and knit together by what every joint supplies, according to the effective working by which every part does its share, causes growth of the body…..*

*---Ephesians 4:11-12; 14-16 NKJV*

Although the health of the body relies on all parts (members), if life in the Body of Christ is to be sustained these specific parts must first work together in harmony. If the natural body cannot exist with just the heart, the brain, and spinal cord; we must also understand that it is impossible for the Body of Christ to exist with just the pastor, teacher, and or evangelist. There are great benefits to the harmonizing of all of these parts, whether in the natural body or in the spiritual Body of Christ. They all represent the sustenance/nourishment of life from which the health of the body/Body begins.

85

It is vital that we distinguish, understand, and celebrate the roles (functions), relationships, and interaction(s) of each member. Figure 5.2 on the following pages will assist in communicating the effective implementation and harmonization of these five parts (members) within the Body of Christ.

## Five Leadership Gifts of the Body of Christ

| Apostle | Prophet | Evange-list | Pastor | Teacher |
|---------|---------|-------------|--------|---------|
| Oversight. | Foresight. Acts 21:8-14 | | | Insight |
| *First in order in the church. 1 Corinthians 12:29* | Second in order in the church. 1 Corinthians 12:29 | Bearers of glad tidings. | Shepard to the sheep. | Third in order in Church. I Corinthians 12:29 |
| *Founding & establishing churches on sure foundation. Ephesians 2:20-22* | Exhortation & confirmation Ezra 5:1, Acts 15:22 | Passion for soul-saving ministry. Proverbs 14:25 | Goes before his sheep. | Student of the Word. I Timothy 4:13 |
| *Ordination and appointmen t of Ministries. Acts 6:1-6* | Has Divine revelation concerning the church. Ephesians 3:1-5 | Fishers of men. | Protects his sheep. | Meditates much. |

| | | | | |
|---|---|---|---|---|
| *Preparation & placing of other* | Foundational ministry along | | | |
| | with the apostles. | Great wisdom in winning souls. | Feeds his sheep. Acts 20:17 | Always teachable. 1 Cor 2:13 |
| *potential ministries. 2 Tim 2:2* | apostles. Ephesians 2:20 | | | |
| | | | | |
| *Church judgments and disciplines. 1 Corinthians 4:21* | | Compelling ministry to the lost. | Connects with the teacher. | Reproduces other teachers. 2 Timothy 2:2 |
| | | | | |
| *Vision for the whole Body of Christ.* | | | Focus on individual Believers. | Judged by God greater than hearers. James 3:1 |
| | | | | |
| *Future advancing.* | | | Maintenance Oriented. | Connects with the Pastor. |
| | | | | |
| *Ability to minister in all of the other five-fold ministries.* | | | | |

| | | | | |
|---|---|---|---|---|
| Foundation ministry along with the Prophet in the church. Ephesians 2:20 | | | | |
| Missional Oriented. | | | | |
| | | | | |

**Figure 5.2**

Emphasis must now be placed on how these members are to interact one with another to form an effective and healthy church.   From the chart in Figure 5.2, it is simple to see that each of the leadership gifts when coordinated one with another can more effectively maintain the healthy functioning of the entire body.   What church would not desire to have gifts (apostles) that could provide oversight and to serve with the love of a father to not only have vision for the local church but for the entire Body of Christ? What leader would not welcome the gifts (prophets) that could hear the voice of God and provide foresight to inevitably forewarn and forearm the Body of Christ in the direction that they are to take?   Who would reject having the gifts (evangelists) that provide motivation, encouragement, and wisdom in gaining souls for the Kingdom of God?   Although more readily accepted and definitely still needed; what would a church do without the gifts (teachers) that provide insight into God's Word and has the ability to communicate them in a very practical and relevant way? How could anyone imagine the church without the gifts (pastors) that provide protection for the sheep and maintains a more personal relationship with individual believers?

God has never intended for his Body/people to operate independent of one another. Every member/gift of the Body must be in its place in order for it to be a fully functional and healthy body/church. Ephesians 4 verse 16 states,

> *from whom the whole body, joined and knit together by what every joint supplies, according to the effective working by which every part does its share, causes growth of the body......*
>
> *---Ephesians 4:16 NKJV*

The bible makes it plain that we are a team. According to Colossians 4:11, we are fellow workers unto the kingdom of God. Because it takes every part, each gift must join together in submission to one another in order to attain the common goal of reaching the unity of the faith. Kevin Conner in his book, "The Church in the New Testament" states, "A team is a group of persons joined together in the same mind, speaking the same thing and going in the same direction."[42]     This same concept is demonstrated and reflected in the Godhead. The Father, Son, and the Holy Spirit each have a distinctive ministry and function but yet all are unified in mind, will, and purpose. Although there is plurality, there is still co-equality and unity. And so it must be with the church if we are to ever attain the measure of the fullness of Christ. We must denounce anything and everything that has the potential to threaten our quest for unity such as: titles, positions, status, and the love of money. We must learn how to respect the differences and celebrate the diversities of our gifts. If the Body is to serve its purpose in the earth, it must grow up into the Head who is the personification of perfection (Divinity). Because of His perfection, it is imperative that His Body (the church) also function as a complete and whole healthy Body. We must understand that when each member of the Body of Christ is effectively operating, its' divinely organized anatomy enables the Body to perform a wide variety of life-sustaining activities, including fighting off the enemy, digesting the milk and meat of God's Word, growing to maturity, and thereby being positioned to fulfill its' mandate to reproduce and/or make disciples of all nations.

## _S i x_

## Making the Shift

### The Healing is in the Body

When the systems of the body are in place and fully functioning, not only does the body have the ability to maintain its health and fight off illnesses, but also a natural capacity to heal itself. According to medical science, the human body completely renews itself every 7 years. The cornea replaces itself every 24 hours, the skin every 14 days, the blood cells every 90 days, the soft tissue every 6 months, and the dense tissue every 2 to 7 years. When the human body encounters a disease or infection it produces complex protein molecules called antibodies to seek out and destroy the invaders.[43] When the body is unhealthy at the start, it sometimes requires substances called "antibiotics" which simulates what is needed by the body in order to help it heal. On the other hand, when the body is whole and healthy it is designed to automatically know how and when to supply what is needed in order to heal itself. When we become sick, the common approach in our natural world is to seek out those substances (antibiotics) that simulate what is needed rather than to seek out and overcome what hinders the natural capacity of our body being positioned to heal itself.

As it is in the natural body, so it is in the Body of Christ. It is quite evident that the Body of Christ has encountered disease and infection. God has also designed the Body of Christ with a natural capacity to heal itself. Ephesians 4:16 says:

*He keeps us in step with each other. His very breath and blood flow through us, nourishing us so that we will grow up healthy ......*

-----Ephesians 4:16 MSG

*He makes the whole body fit together perfectly. As each part does its own special work, it helps the other parts grow, so that the whole body is healthy.....*

-----Ephesians 4:16 NLT

When every member of the body is restored and each gift is fully functioning the Body of Christ will be positioned to automatically know how to and when to supply the necessary antibodies that will seek out and destroy any and everything that tries to invade.

Just as we have adopted the world's leadership structure, we have also adopted the world's approach of seeking out substances (10 step approach, 5 guarantees, 7 ways to overcome, etc.) that simulate what is needed rather than seeking out and overcoming what really hinders the natural capacity of the Body of Christ being able to heal itself. It is for this reason that this chapter will not serve as another how-to manual, but instead will focus on the possible hindrances to the Body of Christ being restored to health and positioned to heal itself.

**Building through the Shift**

We should note throughout the many different moves of God in restoration each move had its challenges and successes which made its impact within the church today. Because God is a builder, He is also using each move in restoration to get us to the place that He originally designed for His people (the church) to be. The place where the equipping/leadership gifts -the apostolic, prophetic, evangelistic, pastoral, and teaching- as well as all the gifts of the Holy Spirit are once again operating in full unity and positioned to grow up into Him. Many within the Body of Christ are beginning to sense that there is a shifting in the atmosphere and that this shifting is going to propel us into places that we have never been nor seen before in Christ. With this shift my greatest concern has been for existing church structures rather than for the emerging leaders. Sure emerging leaders are faced with resisting the temptation of conforming to the usual systems of superiority, but existing leaders are faced with many hindrances that must be overcome if they are ever to make the shift. Among the many, the most difficult hindrances are: fear of the people, losing associations, and hearts that are not totally surrendered and committed to God's order.

**Fear of the People**

"People resist change" is a module of management training that brings awareness to the natural response of people when they are challenged to forego their normal routines in life. It is no different in the church. Unfortunately, due to the level of dependency that has been created by our current leadership structures, the shift for some people may be as challenging as the shift for some of the leaders. Bishop Miller comments, "If restoration is to take place, we must bring people to a willingness to accept change." [44] Leaders must master the ability to be longsuffering with the people, but at the same time challenge them by emphasizing the significance and the necessity of their contribution to the Body. Miller advises, "Be strategic in how you teach it to your congregation. People must be established in the truth. Do not be afraid of their faces. Reaction is certain, but persistence will ultimately win the day." [45]

**Loss of Associations**

Many leaders have developed relationships and associations with denominations, other leaders, and even with partnering churches that could also cause hindrances to restoration of existing church structures. Unfortunately, there is no guarantee that the decision of leaders who are determined to make the shift will be supported by those that are close to them. Some leaders may lose relationships, face disassociations, and even lose financial support. However, the outcome of a fully restored Body and the desire to see things done God's way must be the overriding goal even in the face of such opposition. Nicodemus was a Pharisee (one of the ones that Jesus rebuked) who came to Jesus by night when no one was around because of His associations.[46]

He recognized Jesus as being sent by God to establish God's new order in the earth. However, because he was a member of the Jewish ruling council (one in authority who could have taken a stand on behalf of God's restoration process and possibly made a significant impact on others like him), he decided (for fear of the loss of associations) to continue in support of the old order and remain associated with the Pharisees until the establishment of God's new order and Jesus' work was finished.[47]

*Nicodemus, who had first come to Jesus at night, came now in broad daylight carrying a mixture of myrrh and aloes, about seventy-five pounds. They took Jesus' body and, following the Jewish burial custom, wrapped it in linen with the spices. There was a garden near the place he was crucified, and in the garden a new tomb in which no one had yet been placed. So, because it was Sabbath preparation for the Jews and the tomb was convenient, they placed Jesus in it.*

----John 19:39-42

Leaders must be prepared to stand even in the face of opposition from those closest to them. They must resolve to not just recognize God's order in the Body being restored, but to become an active part of the restoration process.

**Uncommitted Hearts**

I pray that by now leaders hearts are stirred to action in assuring that God's order will prevail in their churches despite the cost. It is my prayer that seeing the benefits of restoration of the Body of Christ back to a fully functioning healthy Body would serve to overcome all levels of selfishness, pride, egotism, conceit and even fear. However, the reality of it is that there will be a struggle against the familiar leadership structures and the tendency to regress. The willingness and desire to see the restoration process through must be more than just a motivational temporary experience. It must be a revelation that comes through your spirit that will enable you to overcome the temptations and desires to relapse into the common form of leadership. We must face the fact that leaders must be able to overcome temptations of superiority, positions, power, status, and money. Bishop Miller states, "There has to be a sense of security and encouragement to be willing to step out of the norm. It must be a revelation that comes into their spirit to allow them to see beyond a paycheck. We must not see God's order as the struggle of anyone trying to get to the top, but rather see it as the foundation on which the Body of Christ stands."[48]

Overcoming those things that hinder the health of the Body of Christ (and even in the natural body) may sometimes be accompanied by pain. However, through true commitment, proper digestion of the Word, a little exercise, and great tips from the World's Greatest Trainer, the Body of Christ will see that 'the pain is worth the gain.'

## Seven

### The Outcome

Rick Joyner in his book "The Apostolic Ministry" writes, "All of the ministries and gifts are but aspects of Christ that He demonstrated when He walked the earth in the flesh. They are demonstrated in the church because He still dwells among us by the Holy Spirit. The functioning of any gift/ministry is actually the moving of Christ within our midst. If we limit any of the gifts or ministries, we are rejecting that aspect of Christ. If the church is going to be all that we have been called to be, we must open our hearts to all of Him."[49] Until now, most of the leadership in our churches has only accepted select aspects of Christ. The outcome has been as it was in the days of Saul, whose leadership enabled the people to fight *some of the battles* of the Lord and accomplish *some things* for God's people but failed to position them to carry the full weight and responsibility of God's people for long.

If the mandate of the Church is to be fulfilled, leaders must make the decision to receive *all* of Him. When this takes place, the outcome according to Ephesians chapter 4 will result in:

- The saints being equipped

    -God's people will no longer walk in defeat and feel inferior but will be equipped and empowered to overcome and rise above any tactic that the enemy may bring.

- The work of ministry being carried out

    -God's people will begin to realize their purpose and become engaged in fulfilling it.

    -Their lives will be fulfilling and the church will be well equipped with those who are now able to be released to do the work of ministry.

-Leaders will be better positioned to target the masses with the gospel without the worry of resources and/or burnout.

- The Body of Christ being edified

   -The Body of Christ will be exposed to more diversified forms of edification which will foster stronger relationships and even greater Spiritual growth.

- God's people reaching the unity of the faith and knowledge of the Son of God

   -God's people will be united on one accord and be a stronger force for impact in the earth.

- The measure of the stature of the fullness of Christ being attained

   -God's people will begin to take on the Characteristics of Christ and become even more visible in the earth.

- God's people reaching maturity

  -No longer will God's people be tossed to and fro by every wind of doctrine, but will instead be able to stand firm and steadfast on God's Word and His ways.

  -The Body will now be positioned to grow up into the Head.

- The Body of Christ growing up in all things into Him who is the Head—Christ,

  -The Body (humanity) will once again reconnect with the Head (Divinity) who is Christ and begin to experience the full manifestation of His presence like never before.

  -In His presence and by His power we will do even greater things (THE MORE OF GOD) than He did just as He promised in John 14:12 (*"Verily, verily, I say unto you,*

> *He that believeth on me, the works that I do*
> *shall he do also; and greater works than*
> *these shall he do; because I go unto my*
> *Father*".

- The growth of the body (as each member does its'
  part)

  -When the environment (garden) is
  restored, the Body of Christ will begin
  to fulfill God's first commandment (to be
  fruitful and multiply/reproduce) and Jesus'
  last command (to go make disciples
  /reproduce) because we are humble,
  obedient and submitted to doing God's
  Work, God's Way.

## *E I g h t*

### Summary and Conclusion

It is evident that God is calling His church to move beyond the place of ineffectiveness and strive to move toward maturity and ultimately discipleship. If the people are to get there, there must be a shifting in the existing leadership structure. Some would argue that the shifting to God's order of leadership is not important and continue to believe that the church is being effective as long as there are people continuing to attend their churches. While compelling them to come is the beginning, we must know that our mandate far exceeds getting people into the church and/or even them getting saved. "The Great Commission is not just to draw numbers or even to make converts, but to make disciples."[50] The church's role is to see that Jesus is formed in the lives of His people to the point where they become like Him. We must know that true success is not measured by the number of people we have in our churches, but rather by the number of disciples we are sending out.

## The Struggle for Strategy

Leaders have been consumed with strategies that assist in building their churches, but in the process have neglected to focus on building the people within those churches. In an article titled "Church Leaders Emphasize Motivation, But Struggle with Strategy" George Barna points out, that while a large percentage of pastors contend that they are gifted at motivating people, 86% percent of pastors struggle with strategy when leading God's people.[51] It is this struggle for strategy that has resulted in the unbalanced extremes of our churches today. In an effort to sustain motivation within and among the people, some of our churches have chosen to lean heavily on the spiritual aspects of Christ. They captivate their audience by focusing on the supernatural to stimulate encounters that suggest relationship. Other churches have chosen to lean heavily on the relational aspects of Christ and captivate their audience by focusing on the practical and being relevant in their teaching. They neglect strategy that will challenge the people to desire deeper levels in their spiritual walk with Christ. Both extremes have managed to draw people but have proven ineffective at making disciples. At this superficial level of Christianity, the people have developed a dependency on leaders who appear to be close to God rather than develop a personal relationship with Him themselves. Many leaders have claimed ownership of their positions in leading God's people due in part, to the amount of effort and energy needed to maintain motivation within people and due in part to the need to feel significant. Church leaders fail to understand that it is by God's grace that they were freely given the gift of leadership and should therefore freely lead God's people, God's way. They have elected to exercise the common form of leadership dictated by our culture which endorses systems of superiority. It is this form of leadership that is now responsible for the lack of involvement from God's people in the work of ministry. Through inferiority generated by systems of superiority, God's people are forced to believe that they have to attain a certain level (within the hierarchy) before they can ever make any significant contribution to the Body of Christ. Instead they resolve themselves to continue to attend church(s), and sit quietly in the pew without ever pursuing God's purpose for their lives. They continue to lead lives that are unchallenged and unfulfilled because they never realize their purpose.

This form of leadership has also caused the lack of accountability and integrity among our leaders. Rather than seeking to serve God's people, many leaders are seeking status, positions, titles, money and power. As the Pharisees did in Jesus' day, many leaders have fallen in love with important seats in the church, places of honor at banquets, being greeted by titles, and large numbers. Our leaders must not continue to judge the success of their church based on nickels and noses when the fact remains that the church's mandate (to make disciples) is not being fulfilled. There are a variety of things that leaders in the church do not agree on; however, any leader who has the heart of God at the center of their ministry must accept that the Body of Christ cannot fulfill the Great Commission in our current condition. The church must experience transformation and it must begin with our existing leadership structure.

**Struggle No more**

The strategy struggle that leaders face in leading God's people is because there is only one strategy that has been designed by God to assure our success at accomplishing the goal of making disciples. Although leaders say it all the time "If God has called us to it, He has made the provisions to see us through it", it is questionable whether most believe it. God has called us to make disciples in the earth, and you best believe that He has also given us the plan to carry it out. Jesus modeled the plan perfectly and we must now follow His example despite our own wisdom and creative leadership abilities. If we are to be successful at being the church, we must begin with leading God's people God's way.

To assure success, Jesus gave each of us gifts that all play a role within the Body of Christ. Verse 7 in Ephesians 4 states, "to each one of us grace was given according to the measure of Christ's gift" in other words, Christ Himself decided who would play what role in the Body; but placed equal significance on each role (grace was given to us all). When the body is unhealthy, it is usually the result of a certain body part (gift) failing to perform its function thereby causing other related systems to malfunction. Although the body may continue its existence without certain parts (gifts), in this condition it is prone to: infections, lack of growth, stunted growth, immaturity, and lack of reproduction. Still there are other parts of the body, if absent or failing to perform their function, will not only cause its related system(s) to malfunction but could cause the entire body to malfunction. Under these circumstances, the body would eventually cease all of life's activities and the end result is death. These parts of the body inevitably are responsible for assuring that everything properly flows (the equipping parts). According to Ephesians 4:11, in the Body of Christ these represent the apostle, prophet, evangelist, pastor, and teacher. "Jesus embodied the Apostle, Prophet, Evangelist, Pastor, and Teacher. When He ascended He gave aspects of His ministry to many. Together these five equipping/leadership gifts formed His complete ministry which was required to equip His disciples and cause them to grow up in all aspects into Him. It is therefore apparent

115

that the church will never become all that it is called to be until all of these gifts are functioning together."[52] Although the health of the body relies on all parts (members), if the life of the church is to be sustained, it must begin with restoration and harmonization of the equipping gifts within the Body of Christ. When each part (member) of the Body of Christ is effectively operating, its divinely organized anatomy will enable the Body to perform a wide variety of life-sustaining activities including: fighting off the enemy, digesting the milk and meat of God's Word, growing to maturity, and thereby being positioned to fulfill the mandate to reproduce and/or make disciples of all nations.

**The Appeal**

Discipleship or Deception was not intended to serve as another " how- to" manual (antibiotic), but rather to bring consciousness to the real condition of the church, while revealing the source of what has caused the Body of Christ to become unhealthy and ineffective. It is my prayer that this manuscript would serve as a clarion call to those who have been entrusted with leading God's people.

Though the message of Discipleship or Deception is contrary to the more commonly accepted method of leading God's people, it is my plea that we "recognize what God has set in the Church rather than continue to reorganize what He has already established."[53]    Just before Jesus was led to die on the cross He prayed this prayer for all who would believe in Him, "May they be brought to complete unity to let the world know that you sent me and have loved them even as you have loved Me."[54] If the world is to ever know Jesus, those who say they represent Him must begin by uniting His Body and allowing God's only **method to maturity** and **strategy for Discipleship** to take us "from where we are (Deception), to where we must go (Discipleship)". Submitting in humility and obedience to Doing God's Work God's Way!

# Endnotes

1. Ephesians. 4.13-15 New Living Translation Bible.

2. Ephesians. 4. 15 King James Version Bible.

3. Ephesians. 4. 11-13 New International Version Bible.

4. George Barna, "Pastors Feel Confident in Ministry, But Many Struggle in their Interaction with Others", July 10, 2006, <http://www.barna.org/FlexPage.aspx?Page=BarnaUpdates> (9 December 2006).

5. George Barna, "Only Half Of Protestant Pastors Have A Biblical Worldview", January 12, 2004, <http://www.barna.org/FlexPage.aspx?Page=BarnaUpdates> (9 December 2006).

5b. George Barna, "A Biblical Worldview Has a Radical Effect on a Person's Life", December 1, 2003 <http://www.barna.org/FlexPage.aspx?Page=BarnaUpdates> (9 December 2006).

6. George Barna, "Number of Unchurched Adults Has Nearly Doubled Since 1991", May 4, 2004, <http://www.barna.org/FlexPage.aspx?Page=BarnaUpdates> (9 December 2006).

7. George Barna, "Spirituality May Be Hot in America, But 76 Million Adults Never Attend Church", March 20, 2006,

http://www.barna.org/FlexPage.aspx?Page=BarnaUp dates (9 December 2006).

8. Barna George, <u>Grow Your Church from the Outside In</u> (Ventura, California: Gospel Light Publications, 2004.

8b. George Barna, "<u>The Concept of Holiness Baffles Most Americans</u>", February 20, 2006, <http://www.barna.org/FlexPage.aspx?Page=BarnaU pdates> (9 December 2006).

9. Bishop Tony Miller, lecture notes for Leading Large Churches, Southwestern Christian University, Greenville, SC., May 18, 2005.

10. Ephesians. 4. 3a <u>King James Version Bible</u>.

11. Genesis. 1. 28 <u>King James Version Bible</u>.

12. Matthew. 28. 18 <u>New King James Version Bible</u>.

13. Romans. 8. 9 <u>King James Version Bible</u>.

14. Bishop Tony Miller, lecture notes for Leading Large Churches, Southwestern Christian University, Greenville, SC., May 18, 2005.

15. Bishop Tony Miller, lecture notes for Leadership Administration, Southwestern Christian University, Atlanta, GA., January 30, 2006.

16. Matthew. 12.2, 12.24, 15.1, 16.1, 16.12, 21.35, 22.15, 22.34 New International Version Bible.

17. Matthew. 16. 5b & 12 New Living Translation Bible.

18. Matthew. 22. 41-46 New Living Translation Bible.

19. Matthew. 23. 2-3 New King James Version Bible.

20. Matthew. 23. 4-7 New King James Version.

21. Matthew. 23. 8-11 New Living Translation Bible.

22. Ephesians. 4.13 New Living Translation Bible.

23. 2 Corinthians. 3.17 King James Version.

24. Shaffer Glenn, Apostolic Government in the 21st Century (Claremore, Oklahoma:)

25. I Samuel. 5. 4-7 New Living Translation Bible.

26. Miles Monroe, In Pursuit of Purpose (Shippensburg, Pennsylvania: Destiny Image Publications, 1992)

27. Rick Warren, The Purpose Driven Life (Grand Rapids, Michigan: Zondervan Publications, 2002)

28. Miles Monroe, In Pursuit of Purpose (Shippensburg, Pennsylvania: Destiny Image Publications, 1992)

29. Jeremiah. 1.5 King James Version.

30. Miles Monroe, In Pursuit of Purpose (Shippensburg, Pennsylvania: Destiny Image Publications, 1992)

31. Matthew. 23.8 New Living Translation Bible.

32. Matthew. 23.3 New Living Translation Bible.

33. Mark. 9.35 King James Version.

34. J. Lee Grady, "Charisma +Online" Fire In My Bones: It's Getting Really Weird Out There, n.d., <http://www.fireinmybones.com/Columns/111105.html > (11 November 2005).

35. I Timothy. 6.6-10 New Living Translation.

35. Matthew. 23. 3b New Living Translation.

37. Miles Monroe, Rediscovering The Kingdom (Shippensburg, Pennsylvania: Destiny Image Publications, 2004)

38. Ephesians. 4.6 New King James Version.

39. Rick Joyner, The Apostolic Ministry (Wilkesboro, North Carolina: Morning Star Publications, 2004)

40. Bishop Tony Miller, interview by Samiour Patterson, MAPS I Project, Southwestern Christian University, 3 March 2006 .

41. <http://encarta.msn.com/encyclopedia_761560 628/Anatomy.html> "Anatomy" <MSN Encarta>

42. Kevin Conner, The Church in the New Testament (Portland, Oregon: City Bible Publishing, 1982)

43. <http://news.bbc.co.uk/1/hi/health/3658582.stm > "Body can 'heal dementia itself' " 16 September 2004, <BBC News>

44. Bishop Tony Miller, interview by Samiour Patterson, MAPS I Project, Southwestern Christian University, 3 March 2006 .

45. Bishop Tony Miller, interview by Samiour Patterson, MAPS I Project, Southwestern Christian University, 3 March 2006.

46. John. 3. 1-2 New International Version.

47. John. 19. 39 -42 New International Version.

48. Bishop Tony Miller, interview by Samiour Patterson, MAPS I Project, Southwestern Christian University, 3 March 2006 .

49. Rick Joyner, The Apostolic Ministry (Wilkesboro, North Carolina: Morning Star Publications, 2004)

50. Rick Joyner, The Apostolic Ministry (Wilkesboro, North Carolina: Morning Star Publications, 2004)

51. George Barna, "Church Leaders Emphasize Motivation, But Struggle with Strategy", February 27, 2006, <http://www.barna.org/FlexPage.aspx?Page=BarnaU pdates> (9 December 2006).

52. Rick Joyner, The Apostolic Ministry (Wilkesboro, North Carolina: Morning Star Publications, 2004)

53. Glenn Shaffer, Apostolic Government in the 21$^{st}$ Century (Claremore, Oklahoma:)

54. John. 17. 23 New International Version.

# Bibliography

Barna, George. "Pastors Feel Confident in Ministry, But Many Struggle in their Interaction with Others", July 10, 2006, <http://www.barna.org/FlexPage.aspx?Page=BarnaUpdates> (9 December 2006).

Barna, George. "Only Half Of Protestant Pastors Have A Biblical Worldview", January 12, 2004, <http://www.barna.org/FlexPage.aspx?Page=BarnaUpdates> (9 December 2006).

Barna, George. "A Biblical Worldview Has a Radical Effect on a Person's Life", December 1, 2003 <http://www.barna.org/FlexPage.aspx?Page=BarnaUpdates> (9 December 2006).

Barna, George. "Number of Unchurched Adults Has Nearly Doubled Since 1991", May 4, 2004, <http://www.barna.org/FlexPage.aspx?Page=BarnaUpdates> (9 December 2006).

Barna, George. "Spirituality May Be Hot in America, But 76 Million Adults Never Attend Church", March 20, 2006, <http://www.barna.org/FlexPage.aspx?Page=BarnaUpdates> (9 December 2006).

Barna, George. Grow Your Church from the Outside In (Ventura, California: Gospel Light Publications, 2004.

# Bibliography

Barna, George. "The Concept of Holiness Baffles Most Americans", February 20, 2006,

<http://www.barna.org/FlexPage.aspx?Page=BarnaU pdates> (9 December 2006).

Shaffer, Glenn. Apostolic Government in the 21st Century . Claremore, Oklahoma:

Monroe, Miles. In Pursuit of Purpose . Shippensburg, Pennsylvania: Destiny Image Publications, 1992.

Warren, Rick. The Purpose Driven Life . Grand Rapids, Michigan: Zondervan Publications, 2002.

Grady, J. Lee. "Charisma +Online" Fire In My Bones: It's Getting Really Weird Out There. n.d. < http://www.fireinmybones.com/Columns/111105.html> (11 November 2005).

Monroe, Miles. Rediscovering The Kingdom. Shippensburg, Pennsylvania: Destiny Image Publications, 2004.

Joyner, Rick. The Apostolic Ministry .Wilkesboro, North Carolina: MorningStar Publications, 2004.

Miller, Tony. Interview by Samiour Patterson. MAPS I Project . Southwestern Christian University, 3 March 2006 .

<http://encarta.msn.com/encyclopedia_761560628/Anato
my.html> "Anatomy", <msn Encarta>

Conner, Kevin. The Church in the New Testament
.Portland, Oregon: City Bible Publishing, 1982.

<http://news.bbc.co.uk/1/hi/health/3658582.stm > "Body
can 'heal dementia itself' " 16 September 2004. <BBC
News>

Barna, George. "Church Leaders Emphasize
Motivation, But Struggle with Strategy", February 27,
2006,
<http://www.barna.org/FlexPage.aspx?Page=BarnaU
pdates> (9 December 2006).

Shaffer, Glenn. Interview by Samiour Patterson.
MAPS I Project . Southwestern Christian University, 27
February 2006.

# The Author's Page

About the Author:

Samiour is a preacher's kid whose desire is to simply pursue and see of the more of God. (John 14:12) He enjoys people, loves leaders, and has a passion to see others grow in their relationship with Christ. Samiour's past experiences has allowed him to serve the Body of Christ in various roles and capacities. He loves music and gardening. His education includes a Master's of Ministry degree in Church Leadership from Southwestern Christian University, a B.S. degree in Organizational Management from Crichton Bible College and an A.S. degree in Computer Science Technology from State Technical Institute. His professional experience includes over 28 years of in-depth analysis, design, development, and implementation in the field of software engineering.

Samiour and his lovely wife Christene have five beautiful children and make their home in Frisco, TX.

Contact the Author:

Samiour L. Patterson

P.O. Box 2681

Frisco, TX 75034

contact@discipleshipordeception.com

discipleshipordeception.com